Radcliffe

IN OLD PHOTOGRAPHS

Radcliffe

IN OLD PHOTOGRAPHS

JOHN HUDSON

Budding
BOOKS

A Budding Book

This book was first published in 1994 by
Sutton Publishing Limited
Phoenix Mill · Thrupp
Stroud · Gloucestershire · GL5 2BU

This edition first published in 2001 by
Budding Books, an imprint of
Sutton Publishing Limited

British Library Cataloguing
in Publication Data. A catalogue record for
this book is available from the British Library.

ISBN 1 84015 219 2

Typeset in 9/10 Sabon.
Typesetting and origination by
Sutton Publishing Limited.
Printed in Great Britain by
J.H. Haynes & Co. Ltd, Sparkford.

Contents

Introduction

I once heard it argued that towns the size of Radcliffe – 25,000 souls or so in the inter-war years – had the very worst of the Industrial Revolution and its aftermath. Their fate in life was all of the muck but not too much of the brass. A collection of pictures such as this can tell only part of the story, but it seems to me that on the evidence of these photographs, the 'missing out' theory is rather too cynical and pessimistic.

There were times this century – and on a lesser scale it is true to this day – when Radcliffe was home to companies whose names were known throughout the world, not just in cotton but equally in engineering, chemicals and paper making. Neighbouring Bury, because it is larger, is often cited as a town on the Manchester fringes that kept on a more even keel than many through the diversity of its industries, but acre for acre, it was even more the case in Radcliffe. Look at the shop window displays in this book, photographed in the depths of the depression in the 1930s, and you see just the tip of an iceberg of local traders who saw the town's needs extending far beyond bread and potato hash.

Not too much of the brass? At the top of Stand Lane from the earliest days of the Industrial Revolution there lived people who had made it big in Manchester, the great vibrant Cottonopolis just down the road, and many of them saw it as a social compulsion to pump their money into the local economy by supporting their neighbourhood shops. But more than this, if you were in work – if you and your wife and four of your children were in the mills, down to the half-time girls of twelve – you were a very inefficient manager indeed if poverty was a problem for you. We look at some of these pictures and we see filth, dilapidated property and evidence of life restricted by geographical and social boundaries. But it is at our peril that we confuse these limitations on our forefathers' lifestyle with hardship as they would have understood the word.

Let us set aside comparisons of relative happiness. It is up to each of us to find ease and peace of mind where we can, and if we are less capable of doing it now than we were fifty years ago, that is more of a reflection on us than on the changing times. Certainly, by almost every objective judgment it is possible to apply, the quality of life available to us today is almost ridiculously superior to what we had to endure in the past. Look at the North Street flood picture on page 50, and ignoring the damage, let the decoration of the house take you back to how we lived forty or fifty years ago. This is one vital area of life, among so many, in which it is hard to believe that many of us would wish to turn back the clock.

Where Radcliffe does miss out today is on a communal sense of destiny. The workmen and the JCBs fiddle away in the town centre, beautifying here and urban renewing there, but how many residents truly believe that these undoubted improvements will bring renewed vigour and prosperity? At least when we and our forefathers were rocked in the cradle of the Industrial Revolution we knew that the rest of the world looked on our lives, scurrying to and from the mills in a permanent coal smoke haze, with a mixture of horror and fascination; but at least the rest of the world looked, and the ground rules were clear to all. Radcliffe was a town dedicated to manual work, take it or leave it. And if you took it you made the best of it with your neighbours in whichever part you happened to live, building your social life around the church, the chapel, the pub, the allotment, the football team, night classes, amateur theatricals, picture shows, public lectures.

Even into the 1960s, it was possible to take almost for granted that your little town, known to scarcely anyone beyond the Manchester area, and then more often than not confused with the other Radcliffe in Nottinghamshire, should turn its hand to any number of trades and industries. In no particular order, and leaving aside the industrial giants of the town and everyone involved in producing textiles and paper, cast your mind back to Entwistle's pickles and jams, Riley's pop, Lonsdale and Bridge's leather goods, Sweetule toffee cigarettes, Walter Spencer's hats, makers of shuttles and spindles like John Haddock, Tootill and Snape, Hardman and Ramsbottom. Then there was Jones, London and Garrard down at Bankside Mills who were almond millers, for heaven's sake, the Neelys who made cricket bats, the Stopes pottery that turned out chimney cowls. The point is, we did not go around in 1950 saying: 'Isn't it amazing, we live in a town where we make everything from ground almonds to spindles.' We simply took it as read that it was our collective destiny to serve the rest of the country and in many cases the world in this way. And now that certainty has gone, it is not easy to see what will take its place.

One enduring trait in the town is an interest in its roots and heritage – and not surprisingly so, since what happened to Radcliffe and the other mill towns really was extraordinary. Today, and presumably for the rest of time, life in small town Lancashire goes on and will go on much as it does in small town

Leicestershire or Derbyshire, the bypass, the discount warehouses, the sports centre, the video shops. But for 150 years Radcliffe and its peers were complete one-offs in the eyes of the rest of the world, and it is a tradition to be prized. In my choice of photographs for this book I have tried to concentrate on human interest, and hope that I have not offended would-be contributors in doing so. What I have endeavoured to do is avoid good 1934 views of buildings that look like bad 1994 ones. It matters little to me if a shot shows the church tower before the ivy was cut away, or the mill before the 1926 extension was built. Give me the 1920s dance band, the pile of pennies in the pub, the black face minstrels, the bonny babies in Close Park . . .

I hope all who have helped me are acknowledged on page 128, but I trust I shall offend nobody if I single out three for special mention: Diana Sorrigan, for giving me access to a Radcliffe Library collection full of hidden gems from the Halliwell studio in particular; Jim Barlow of Sherwood Avenue for his boundless support and demon detective work; and Rod Launders, whose grassroots enthusiasm for chronicling the visual and written history of Radcliffe Cricket Club will have a positive influence on the Racecourse and those who frequent it for generations to come. That having been said, nobody fed me with more cups of tea, caramel wafers or potato waffles on my forays to Radcliffe than Phyllis Hudson of Whitefield. But then again, isn't that what mums are for?

John Hudson, 1994

SECTION ONE

Blackburn Street
and Stand Lane

Just another day in Radcliffe in around 1926, with the Black Lane tram going about its business in Stand Lane.

A policeman stands in the middle of Blackburn Street in no imminent danger in this tranquil scene from the early 1920s. The Westminster Bank, Maypole's provisions store and Kenyon's tripe shop – far better remembered as the UCP – are among businesses on the left, while on the extreme right is Marks and Spencer's Penny Bazaar. It was the presence of M and S and Woolworth's that helped give Blackburn Street its 'High Street' feel, even though Stand Lane had the biggest store in town in the Co-Operative Emporium.

Timpson's boot and shoe shops were in almost every town, and the company was among the first of the chains to break in on what had at one time been little more than a cottage industry. In this view of the shop at 13 Stand Lane in around 1930, finest quality ladies' dancing shoes are 8s 11d, gents' boots and ladies' autumn lace shoes are just under 13s and South African field boots are described as splendid value at 14s 11d.

The best men's outfitters and hatter's shop in town was Emerson's in Blackburn Street. Its window displays always made the fashion-conscious male look twice, and when it came to buying dad a pair of sock suspenders or a box of collar studs at Christmas, it always made you feel good if you could say you'd got them at Emerson's. Here the shop is looking even more impressive than usual, being dressed up for the chamber of trade's Prosperity Push window display of October 1933. Out in Hollywood, the movie maker Busby Berkeley was trying to sing and dance us out of our depression blues with films like his *Gold Diggers* of that year. Radcliffe could not go quite as glossy as that, but dozens of its shops put on a super show for the Prosperity Push. A few Emerson's prices: cloth caps, 2s 11d; Hoyle's super poplin shirts, 10s 6d; furrow stripe shirts, 5s 6d; ties at 2s 6d; and bowlers from 6s 11d to 12s 6d.

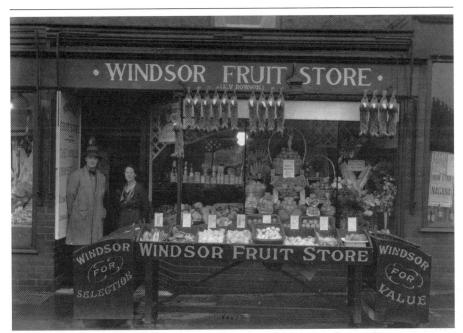

Adjacent shops in Blackburn Street, *c.* 1930: above, the Rowson family's Windsor Fruit Store, and below, Jolley's butchery at No 95. Bananas are 1d each, pears 2d each and apples 3d a pound at the greengrocers, while at the chip shop on the right – where plaice with your penn'orth of chips costs 3d or 4d – the Bridge picture house is advertising its two films for the week, *The Iron Stair* and *Nagana*. Welsh lamb dominates Jolley's window display, with prices at from 9d to 1s 4d a pound.

Stand Lane Shops decorated for Radcliffe Carnival in the early 1900s. On the left, decorated with fans and Chinese lanterns, is the high class grocery shop of Joseph Taylor, a company that had a factory near by making jams and other fruit-based products. An elaborate floral display adorns Hurst's watch maker's and jeweller's shop, while on the right, Wolstenholme's haberdashery was doubtless also putting on an eye-catching show.

Stand Lane in 1961, before they cut off the old Co-Operative Emporium in its prime and disguised its truncated remains as an MFI-style warehouse. Dating from 1877, when 1,300 drank tea and ate cakes to celebrate its opening, the central Co-Op was not an inspiring sight in its later years, but the revival of Victorian warehouses in Manchester and elsewhere has proved that such buildings can look good and play a part in modern life. Across the road, the cheques and pound notes of Martins Bank have now given way to the chianti and pasta of an Italian restaurant. The picture below dates from 1910, the Radcliffe and Pilkington society's 50th anniversary.

Another window from the Prosperity Push of 1933, this time Maypole's in Blackburn Street. Maypole was one of those well-organized chains like Burgon's and Home and Colonial that had the capacity to store and distribute perishables such as butter and bacon, and it is no coincidence that many of today's giant supermarket chains stem from such operations. Maypole prices: margarine from Mayco at 4d to the supreme May-Queen at 1s 1d a pound, New Zealand and Danish butter at 8d a pound, tea at from 1s to the astonishing Mikado Ceylon blend at 2s 4d a pound, and condensed milk at 3d a tin. A similar shop remembered by many was Sherry's, on the corner of Blackburn Street and Deansgate.

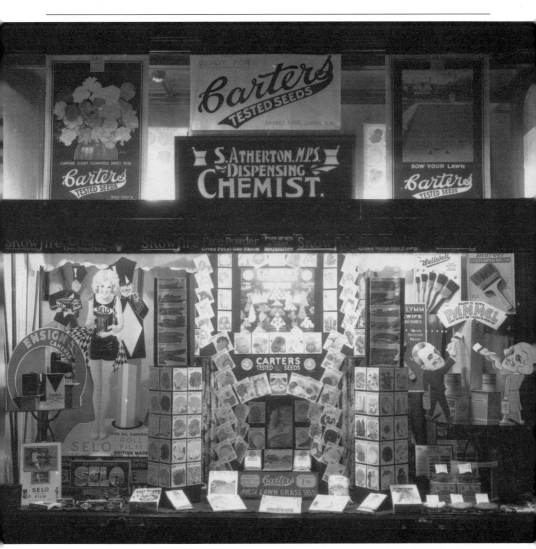

Carters seeds dominate this window display at Atherton's chemist's shop in Stand Lane in around 1930, but there are also eye-catching cardboard advertising cutouts – the kind that command hefty sums on today's nostalgia market – for Ensign cameras, Selo films and Pammel paints. No doubt Atherton's would deal with your prescription with skill and efficiency, too, but at this stage they seemed keen to sugar the pill by emphasizing the more pleasant side of life. The only remotely medical product advertised is Snowfire Face Powder, which apparently gave a 'petal-like bloom' in spite of its somewhat threatening sounding name.

Turner and Booth's, first of Church Street but in Stand Lane in most people's memory, were best known for their radios, but gramophones, Drydex torches and Tempex electric clocks are also on offer in this photograph from *c*. 1933. As can be seen from the top picture opposite, showing one of Turner and Booth's window displays, there was a wealth of Art Deco glamour about early radio. Sets did not come cheap, either. The Philco models seen here range from 12 to 22 guineas, and even if you were doing quite well in life, that could well have been several weeks' wages. The dials were irresistibly alluring, with the delights of Hilversum and Beromunster, Leipzig and Radio-Paris just a turn of the knob away; but the reality was often rather more mundane, and a typical night's listening-in on the National Programme in 1933 might have been a selection of Hungarian light music, a Henry Hall concert, a 15-minute interlude, the news, Major Walter Elliot talking to farmers and a reading of a poem by Walter de la Mare. From 10.35 to midnight, however, life hotted up, with a dance band from a top London nightspot – perhaps Sydney Kyte at the Piccadilly Hotel – giving little towns like Radcliffe a tantalizing glimpse of another world.

Philco fantasy: see opposite for an account of the radio world of Turner and Booth's.

An equally exciting window display? It depends on your excitement threshold. CWS Belmont lingerie and Desbeau corsets feature prominently at the Co-Op's Stand Lane store, *c.* 1930.

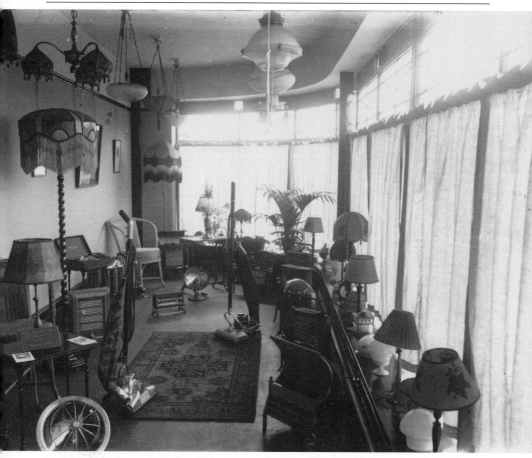

In the heart of town and demolished as part of the central redevelopment, the electricity showrooms were once essential viewing for every home-maker. Here in the upstairs room, *c.* 1930, vacuum cleaners vie for our attention alongside standard lamps with stylish Art Deco beaded shades, heaters and table lamps.

SECTION TWO

Meet the Folks

Local heroes: Radcliffe winners of Royal Humane Society awards in the town from 1900 to 1910, with some very young recipients, including one of the two women. In a world where danger was never far beneath the surface of daily life, in unprotected machinery, canal towpaths, mine shafts, dilapidated buildings and unreliable gas supplies, it was not uncommon for people to be called upon to prove their heroic mettle.

In the days before political correctness, blacking up with burnt cork was a sure-fire way for carnival bands to catch the eye. The Household Jazz Band, seen here, won second prize for their efforts in around 1930. The winners must have put on quite a show.

What a staggering picture this is, a public weigh-in of babies and toddlers at Close Park, *c.* 1930. This was a time of depression, in which sanitary inspectors and medical officers of health were rightly growing increasingly outspoken about the wretched condition of worn-out housing stock in the teeming little streets of damp, dirty towns like Radcliffe. Nevertheless, on a bright afternoon more than 60 summers ago, scores of mothers could turn out in the park for an event like this, cuddling little children as happy and healthy as you could wish to see. Healthy? What's the betting that dozens of them are still very much alive and kicking and enjoying this fascinating little fragment of their early life?

Stars of the Ambulance Drill Hall in Mellor Street, and many a Sunday school hop: those foot-tapping syncopators the Celebrity Boys, whose ages seem to range from late teens to mid-fifties.

St John Ambulance Brigade officials in around 1907, some 20 years after the organization's foundation nationally. Those white sashes and black uniforms are familiar, but there is a far more military air about the group than is apparent today, with three wearing sergeant's stripes, and two corporal's. The commander in the centre appears to be going one better by sporting his Boer War campaign medals.

A well-dressed group in front of the YMCA building at Allens Green bowling club in 1930, among them the long-serving Councillor Jim Henry Hall. Two bowling woods and a jack are placed in the centre foreground, but members of the party scarcely seem ready for sporting action. One woman and a few children have strayed into the picture, one boy wearing a Bury Grammar School cap.

You can almost smell the mothballs: an old folks' Christmas tea party in the 1920s, with fur collars and heavy coats abounding and a cracker for every guest. The banner on the back wall could be more trade union than church, and the mill architecture of the wall and iron pillars suggests that this is probably a works or union treat. The young women helpers in the background are all wearing silly hats, and a single child seems to have gatecrashed with grandma, no doubt to the irritation of other guests: 'I'd have brought our Vera and Jim if I'd known they were lettin' kiddies in.'

Fur coats and sensible boots: opening the Women's Voluntary Service rest centre at the Manse, Walker Street, Chapelfield on what was obviously a wet and rainy June day in 1942. Walker Street and its adjoining Chapel and Union Streets were on the site of today's Chapel Field.

A street outing by Motor Transit Company transport for women of Egerton Street and their neighbours in the 1920s.

Radcliffe and Pilkington Co-Operative Women's Guild members in the 1920s. There were 15 women among the society's founding 181 members in 1860, the first to join, and the 15th overall, being one Elizabeth Howarth. This was a decent enough start for mid-Victorian times, but the old Co-Op remained a male-dominated body, and at the time of its golden jubilee in 1910 it could list not a single woman among the 114 members who had risen to the dizzy heights of committee status over the previous 50 years.

(*Opposite*) John Holt was a dialect poet whose work did the rounds from the 1870s into the early years of this century. His Lancashire poems were unmemorable and his commemorative verses in standard English were awful, far too close for comfort to the dreadful dirges being churned out at the same time by the notorious William McGonagall. A stalwart of the Co-Op movement and Stand Unitarian Church, Holt had his *Occasional Verses* published by friends in 1912. It was not a happy time. One of the better rhymes was shown to be plagiarism and the foreword to the book was an admirable exercise in damning with faint praise by R. Travers Herford, the highly sophisticated and literary Unitarian minister.

Cycle rally, 1950s, and a tense Jacqueline Sandiford of North Street prepares not to knock down any policemen or ride the wrong way round roundabouts.

A dominant force in turn-of-the-century Radcliffe politics, County Councillor J. R. Ragdale played a major role in the town's 1897 Diamond Jubilee and 1902 Coronation celebrations, was president of the Literary and Scientific Society from 1896 to 1898 and was at the heart of negotiations with the benefactor Andrew Carnegie for a £5,000 contribution towards the public library. For such a weighty worthy he looks quite a flamboyant soul with his quiff, luxuriant moustache and lapel rose.

A 1950s Sunday afternoon in Close Park, on a day not so warm as some of the folk who came out without coats might have wished. Apart from the splendid period styles in dresses and motor transport, what strikes one most about this scene is that nobody is actually doing anything other than enjoying the air or talking to their neighbour. No knitting, no newspapers, no books, no radios, not even a letter to write. Few groups of so many people would be so happy with their own company today.

SECTION THREE

Around the Town

'Saturday Penny' is the title the photographer William Kershaw gave to this fine but obviously staged picture of Pickup's shop in Sandford Street in the years before the First World War. It's another scene long gone, for the property was demolished in the 1950s.

Pat Cullen was listed as landlord of the Old Cross Hotel in Cross Lane in 1933, and there is no reason to believe that this is not him with his brood. Joseph Holt's pubs were usually few and far between, with the result that there was never a huge groundswell of enthusiasm for their distinctive products in any one town. Today, the brewery is much beloved of real ale enthusiasts.

The Radcliffe and Pilkington Co-Op is no more, but the building of this fair-sized branch in Bury Street still stands. It is seen here not many years after its opening in 1926, Close Methodist Church looming behind its flat roof.

A wonderful photograph from the Halliwell studio, an unidentified Radcliffe and Pilkington Co-Op butcher's shop. Huge hams, ribs and strings of sausages hang in the windows, and notices urge customers to Join Our Christmas Club and enjoy the benefits of the legendary dividends paid out to members. There were times when these were well worth having. In 1909, for instance, the society had sales of £148,654 – and paid out to its 4,446 members a total of £20,604 in divi.

A little bit of beautifying at Top o' th' Cross in the 1950s. Students of design will recognize the advertisements as typical of around the time of the Festival of Britain and the Coronation.

Everyone in his or her place: one to run the drapery, one the butchery and four the grocer's at the Co-Op in Cross Lane in 1910.

A busy shopping centre for the north end of town: Water Street in around 1907.

When staffing the corner shop was a five-man operation: George Mason's, on the junction of Water Street and Ainsworth Road, in around 1930. Soap and butter were the special deals that week, the former at 5½d and the latter at 2s 1d a pound for Danish and 1s 9d for New Zealand. Irish eggs were also a good buy at 1s 4d a dozen – not that the thought of eggs hanging around quaysides and taking their chance on a slow boat across the Irish Sea has great selling appeal.

This scene from the John and Margaret Fletcher collection shows the Manchester, Bolton and Bury Canal heading north-east towards the Victoria Street footbridge and the Water Street bridge beyond. The boats are almost certainly carrying coal, perhaps en route from Ladyshore colliery to Bury. The MBB Canal Society now takes a vital interest in the future of the canal, and it is hoped that the culvert under Water Street will be replaced by a bridge under which craft can navigate by the early 2000s.

Such a familiar scene a couple of decades ago: down come the houses of the early Industrial Revolution, this time in Eton Hill Road.

The Picturedrome in Water Street in around 1913, when they took their picture palaces seriously. It later became the Rex and was treated with less reverence, but there are still many who believe that even in its latter days as a bingo hall it served the community better than the anonymous patch of green that has taken its place.

Those Co-Op branches get everywhere in this book, as indeed they got everywhere in Radcliffe, to the extent that there were a dozen around the town by 1910. This picture shows the Water Lane branch in that year.

Poor old Bury was rewarded with a mock-up tank made of plywood to mark its contribution to the First World War armament effort. Radcliffe's 'tank' was not a tank but a lighter armoured vehicle; but at least it was real, and it stood in ever-decaying splendour in Coronation Park until even the most patriotic of the town's fathers had seen enough of it and had it scrapped in 1934. Odd to think that if it had survived another half-dozen years it would have been whisked away to help re-arm for another war.

Coronation Park was in the news again in the early 1960s, when two unknown actors named Alan Bates and June Ritchie filmed moody, misty sequences there and along Sailor Brews for the movie *A Kind of Loving*. Mr Bates had a rotten northern accent and went on to become an international superstar. Miss Ritchie, from Stretford, sounded just right and was scarcely seen again. There's no justice, is there?

Filming near Coronation Park again, but this time only for local TV. Down comes Hardcastle's mill chimney just before Christmas in 1974.

Naylor's service station, on the Radcliffe side of the Goat's Gate boundary with Whitefield, *c.* 1930. There's still a garage there, at Radcliffe New Road's junction with Spring Grove.

The end of town around the East Lancashire Paper Mill, seen from the air in 1947. The adjacent cotton mill with a square corner tower, Wilton Mill, was demolished in early 1994 to make way for expansion at the prospering paper mill, which had used it as a store and despatch depot since 1966.

Close to the original St Mary's parish church, with its 13th-century remains, Radcliffe Tower is a ruin at least 600 years old and possibly a great deal older. An official ancient monument since the 1920s, it was part of a great hall and manor house complex until its later adjoining buildings were declared unsafe and pulled down in around 1840. This bleak picture shows the tower in January 1963, a couple of decades before landscaping work gave a more pleasing setting to a little bit of history that has always been something of an embarrassment to the town: it's old, we're proud of it – but what on earth do we do with it?

Archaeological dig at Radcliffe Tower in 1964, with Messrs A. Shawcross and J.A. Barlow taking stock.

Flashback to the 1920s? By no means. This was 'The Shop' in Dumers Lane as recently as the 1950s, though some of its enamel advertising signs go back a decade or two before then.

Trees in blossom and a hen scratching in the yard: Pump Croft Farmhouse, Red Bank, in the early years of this century.

The Grundy family's Oak Cottage, Chapelfield, which was eventually demolished in the late 1950s. There is not much timber and thatch around Radcliffe and houses with possible 16th-century roots are thin on the ground, but the high ground up towards Stand is rich in history, with the Old Hall one of the great lost houses of northern England.

Whittaker Street Baths, with their main pool and 11 slipper baths, were built in 1898 and met this fate in 1971, the camera here pointing towards the shallow end. More would be done to rescue the roof girders' ornamental wrought ironwork if the exercise could be repeated today.

A drama and perhaps even a crisis, but it is hard to untangle quite what went wrong when property was damaged as well as vehicles in this Radcliffe tramway accident of 1916.

Most of this scene was swept away in 1937, very soon after this picture was taken, when the open market to the rear on the left, the central Market Hall and the lock-up shops to the right all gave way to redevelopment. The council truck carries scaffolding from the open market, while a sign beside the shops imposes some of Radcliffe's first parking restrictions.

Bell's Egg Stall, still a familiar name in the market of today, back in 1970. Own-farm eggs are 3s 6d a dozen, delicious crumbly Lancashire cheese is 4s a pound – yet the proprietors still feel the braces-and-belt need to put up a sign saying 'Don't Forget To Buy Your Eggs'. Did chronic amnesiacs really walk at large in Radcliffe a quarter of a century ago?

Factory fires were a part of life. This is at Crow Oak Works, off Radcliffe New Road, in September 1936.

Surveying the disastrous Market Hall fire of 1980, at which the ovenproof qualities of the crockery on the stall to the left were put to a severe test.

Cleaning up flood damage in North Street, 1950s. Even leaving aside the devastation, this rare inside view of a terrace house gives some idea of living conditions for thousands of Radcliffe families until fairly recent times.

Deputy borough surveyor Mr A. Tulip lowers a marsh gas lamp into an old mine shaft discovered during road works at Stopes in 1972.

The first tram to Black Lane, now Ainsworth Road, from the town centre in 1905. The terminus was at Black Lane Bridge, but a giant leap forward came just two years later, when a branch of the Bury–Bolton line came down the hill from Three Arrows.

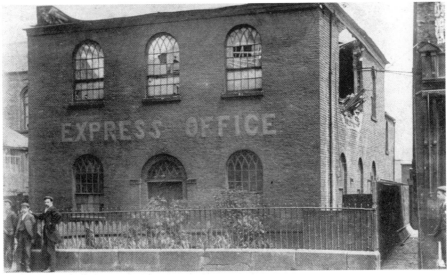

This building in Stand Lane began life as Bridge Methodist Chapel in 1815, went over to commercial use when the fast-expanding congregation built its larger church near by in Milltown Street in 1833, and was demolished in 1906 to make way for the public library which opened there in the following year. From 1883 to 1901 it was the printing works for the weekly *Radcliffe Express*.

Crash, bang, wallop, what a picture: comedian Colin Crompton and regulars at the Turf Hotel in Water Street give a mighty cheer as a pile of pennies topples for charities for the blind in 1979.

Anger in Howard Street, as mothers protest against its use by through traffic in October 1972.

The peace dividend: air raid shelters give way to more positive developments at the East Lancashire Paper Mill in 1947.

The miners' strike of 1972, and pickets at the National Coal Board depot at Outwood Road make their point to a driver for local merchants G. Walker.

Edward Street in the 1950s, soon to be demolished along with so many more under slum clearance orders. A brilliant photograph, but no artistic skill can disguise the mean state of little houses clearly at the end of their natural lifetime.

SECTION FOUR

Happiest Days of their Lives?

War orphaned boys' and girls' outing, early 1920s, with the five large Leyland charas decorated with the flags of the First World War allies, including Japan. It must have been a big day for these youngsters.

Girls of the Radcliffe and Pilkington Co-Op Children's Circle in the 1920s, portraying all nations joining in co-operation.

Surely not the happiest day of Bridge Methodist pupils' lives, the day their school burned down in 1978.

A cheerful little bunch: a junior class at St Paul's Methodist School, later Wesley Methodist, *c.* 1938.

There are no more delightful pictures in this book than these, taken at a film show in the Civic Hall early in 1967. That's not so long ago – but can you imagine today's generation of children, in their video and electronic world, reacting to a screen adventure in such a positive way?

A sale of work at Radcliffe Congregational School in 1927. To the rear are the deacons, some of whom are remembered as Mr and Mrs Hardman, Mr and Mrs Scholes, Mr and Mrs Hargreaves, Mr and Mrs Cannon, Mr and Mrs Fletcher, Mr and Mrs W. Kenyon and Mr and Mrs J. Kenyon.

Congregational School nymphs and shepherds, photographed by the ubiquitous F. Danby of Sion Street, who did his very best for these little children with a classical backdrop and drapes.

The last scholars at St Anne's day school, which served its corner of the town from 1884 until the early 1930s.

St John's School infants in their garden, 1927. There appear to be some rugged individualists among them, and who says teachers of those days did not earn the kind of pay that allowed them to go into retirement with their favourite indulgence, an Austin Seven car? No doubt they felt the need to put some space between themselves and their old working haunts.

Growing up: St John's scholars in 1933, on the verge of going on to secondary school.

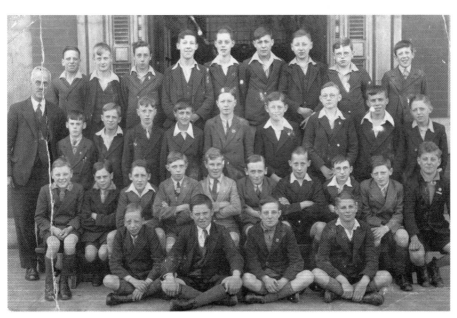

Second year boys at Radcliffe Central Senior School, mid-1930s.

Nearly 70 children were found a role in a musical, *Jan in Windmill Land*, put on by Radcliffe Parish Church School and directed by its well-loved headmaster James Woodhead. For some children, at least, genuine Dutch clogs were found – and several older natives of Radcliffe have gone through life remembering snatches of songs from this event that brought colour and excitement to their young lives.

Radcliffe Congregational School standard three in 1927. Teacher Mr Clay is on the left, headmaster Mr Hulme to the right.

A Co-Op Children's Circle outing in the 1920s, more than 60 girls supervised by just two adults. Doubtless many of the older girls were well used to the role of little mother. Like most Lancashire town children, Radcliffe youngsters were privileged to be in walking distance of safe open country. Truly urban creatures like the inner-city kids of Manchester were the exception rather than the rule.

Transports of Delight

The month is May 1959, and although Radcliffe Central has been modernized, the train is one of the English Electric five-coachers that plied the Bury–Manchester line from 1915 until very shortly after this photograph was taken. The second coach was first class, which seemed an outmoded luxury in the trains' later years.

What excitement: Black Lane station at the beginning of the 1965 wakes, when the demise of the cotton industry and £19 weeks in Majorca had not quite put an end to scenes such as this. A few hours later these folk would be bumping into each other on Blackpool Prom and shrieking: 'We came here to get away from you.'

William Lees of Mellor Street was a general carrier who was one of the first to go into charas in a big way. The destination board is a reminder that even if you couldn't make Blackpool, there was much to be said for a sunny Sunday in Heaton Park.

A Radcliffe Carnival Queen sits pretty in a flower-bedecked landau. What an exciting day for her and her two pageboys, though it's hard to imagine that their powdered wigs stayed the course on such a sunny afternoon.

A children's outing from Joshua Lowe's Unicorn pub on Bolton Road, *c.* 1930, boys in one chara and girls in another, as was often the case. The little boys in the centre of the picture wear peaked school caps, while the slightly older ones sport the cloth cap style that some of them doubtless stayed with for the rest of their lives. The pub is now the Beer Engine – recalling for some older residents the 'engine pits' down nearby Pitt Street, old mine workings where the lads of 60 years ago used to play.

Radcliffe Motor Transit Company was so pleased to supply this Morris van to Joseph Taylor's that it recorded the event for posterity. Taylor's, who had a grocery in Stand Lane and a factory in Mill Street and had a history dating back to 1865, described themselves variously as manufacturers of candied peel and fruit preserves. All very posh – but their premises, inevitably, were known simply as 'the jam works'.

This time it's Pickwick Motors of Stand Lane advertising their wares, and evidently very proud of this Ford six-wheeler supplied to the hauliers H. E. Ormerod.

Builders and timber merchants William Rigby of Radcliffe Saw Mills in Spring Lane were masters of their craft, and had large Burford trucks to prove it. This picture was taken near their works, with the Technical College in Whittaker Street to the left and John Hardman's motor body works, founded 1855, to the right. For many years Hardman's advertised themselves as 'lurry makers', using a genuine though now obsolete spelling of the word that reflected local pronunciation.

'Carnival Spirit' is the theme of this Joseph Taylor float, *c.* 1930. The cart behind is piled high with CWS cocoa.

Carnival time for J. Spencer Ashworth's of Dumers Lane. Their main stock in trade was a range of technical products for the bleaching, dyeing and finishing industries, but they also tried their hand at two 'boons for housewives' under the Spenash label, a liquid washing blue and a washing tablet.

A 1920s CWS carnival float advertises tennis and other summer sports goods. The girls look dashing enough, but skirts are strictly down to the ankle.

The scene is the rear of the old Market Hall, *c.* 1900. Not an auspicious spot, but the beautifully turned out van of Rigg Brothers, the Bolton wholesale confectioners, adds lustre to the humdrum surroundings.

Described as a May Day horse, though some dispute it, this stallion is certainly a picture of good grooming. Judging from the position of the picture, with St Thomas's church in the background, it could well be from Whewell's weaving sheds in York Street, for they were famous for their immaculate horses.

Always a welcome visitor to Radcliffe Fair, showman Pat Collins's Fowler traction engine Lord James.

Products for around the world: the loading bay at the East Lancashire Paper Mill, 1954.

Another promotion, this time for Richard Seed of Seed Street's brewery in a 1920s Shopping Week. The scene is outside the old Market Hall, not far from the brewery's most prestigious hotel, the Boar's Head. You can still see the long-lost Seed's advertised on the tile façade of what was once the main meeting place in town, headquarters of dozens of clubs and societies, but people whose memories do not stretch back so far might recall it more as an 'Oh Be Joyful' Dutton's house.

SECTION SIX

Church Life

An elegant example of Gothic Revival architecture, St Andrew's church, off Ainsworth Road, *c.* 1930. Not much of a day for Whit Walks or anything else, but somehow the rain on the footpath and setts by no means detracts from this atmospheric picture from the Halliwell studio.

St Andrew's Carnival, 1910, viewed from an upstairs window in Ainsworth Road by F. Danby.

One of the most dramatic visual improvements to central Radcliffe in the post-war years has been the cleaning of St Thomas's church in 1972 and the grassing, a dozen years earlier, of its large churchyard. This involved the removal of some 1,200 headstones, with just two left to commemorate the thousands buried there. This picture, showing untended grass, shrubs and blackened gravestones that had once been scrubbed and donkey-stoned by loving relatives of the departed, is a telling reminder of why the move was felt necessary in 1959.

Another major improvement among very many at St Thomas's church in the post-war years was the removal of the by then superfluous side galleries in 1959. This is typical of the shabby scene below them shortly before they went; the equivalent spot today is almost unrecognizable from this photograph.

A painted jewel of a church – but one that exacted a heavy toll on maintenance funds: St Thomas's chancel arch shortly after its restoration in 1914.

The Rev. Robert Fletcher, Vicar of St Thomas's from 1844 to 1890. He graduated from Oxford in 1840 but there was none of the Anglo-Catholic Oxford Movement about him. He was famously low church, hard working and popular with many, not least several Nonconformist ministers in the town with whom he got on splendidly. Even surplices, scarcely the most outrageous religious finery, had no place in the Fletcher wardrobe.

Two Vicars in ninety years. The Rev. Heber Marks, Robert Fletcher's curate, took over St Thomas's on his death in 1890 and stayed until he in turn passed away in 1935. He is best remembered as a man who had two streets named after him while he was still in his prime. Heber and Marks Streets were among four to be built on the church's former glebe land in the 1890s.

The Rev. Sidney Cooke was St Thomas's Vicar from 1935 to 1945, a Midlander who won the Military Cross as a Royal Artillery captain in the First World War. Hundreds of couples who were wed in the town at around the time of the 1939–45 conflict still have Sidney Cooke's signature tucked away on their marriage certificates.

The Rev., now Canon, Reg Smith was Vicar of St Thomas's from 1949 to '59, and has been Rector of Bury for the past 28 years. Born in 1915, he retains the zest for life that saw him double the number of communicants at the Radcliffe church and transform its social life. Outside church he is best known as a witty after-dinner speaker and for his near-miraculous enthusiasm for Bury Football Club.

St John's, Stand Lane, an Anglican rallying point in an area once known as Little Ireland, was consecrated in 1866. It was closed in 1974, when its parish was merged with that of St Thomas, and taken down two years later. A cairn now marks its site.

Dedication service of the redesigned St Thomas's church, which also marked its union with St John's, in November 1974.

Laying the stone at the Hampson Mission, which served the growing Black Moss area of St Thomas's parish off Bolton Road, in August 1912. It opened in 1914, and after a few years became St Philip's church.

The octagonal St Philip's was designed by local architects to serve as both a church and a community hall, but by the late 1950s it was clear that a larger building was needed. Progress was slow, and it was not until March 1975 that the final service was held at the old mission. St Philip's Community Centre now stands on its site.

Wartime brought many changes – one of them the admission, for the first time, of women to the choir of St John's, Stand Lane. Here is the first intake, in their smart mortar boards and cravats, in 1940.

Radcliffe Parish Church choristers on a 1950s Whit Walk.

A Parish Church choir outing to the seaside, late 1950s. A cricket bat was among the luggage, paving the way for sport to unite a rather diverse group of people.

A Whit Walk of the early 1900s. Apart from clothing fashions, little changed in the spirit of the event for generations.

A St John's, Stand Lane, Whit Walk of the 1930s. The raised garden was at the front of George Whewell's furniture removal business.

The colour parties of the Radcliffe Scout troops enter the Parish Church for the St George's Day parade of 1960.

St John's Scouts at the junction of Radcliffe New Road and Stand Lane during a pre-war Whit Walk. This corner, with its towering street lamp landmark, was always a great rallying point on the walks.

Another of those pictures that almost puts you in with the crowd, this time outside the Co-Op general offices in Sion Street, the odd building with large glazed upper rooms now occupied by a bathroom showroom.

All in a Day's Work

Radcliffe fire and ambulance station in Whittaker Street in the early years of the century. The mortuary and town yard were also in this busy corner. Radcliffe was among the first provincial brigades to have a motorized fire tender – some say THE first, though it is always as well to be wary of such superlatives. Early Radcliffe vehicle registration numbers are interesting. They tend to come from here, there and everywhere, Bury, Bolton, Manchester and Salford. In Bury, if someone drove by not sporting an EN plate in the 1920s the natives felt inclined to stop him and ask for his passport.

The fire brigade before the internal combustion engine, but again at Whittaker Street.

The most irritating picture of all, for the compiler, at least. R. S. Howarth's mill furnishers' and sheet metal works was off Whittaker Street, yet behind the firm's rather shack-like premises here is what can only be a cinema with a large sign proclaiming TODAY and another over a side door reading 2d Seats. All very well, but there was no cinema anywhere near Whittaker Street. Just for once, could readers please sort this one out?

Sion Street was one of the first to have tarmac laid, in the 1920s, and the submerging of the setts had a profound effect on the feel and atmosphere of the place, as well as car tyres. On the right is Peel Mill, one of the giants of the Radcliffe industrial scene, while in the distance on the left are the Co-Op's general offices, their rooftop pediment just visible. On its façade it shows a carving of industrious bees around a hive, still there to this day above the bathroom showrooms that occupy the building.

It could be one of a hundred Radcliffe stable yards of the early years of this century, tucked-away red brick and cobbled backwaters where men like these kept the wheels of the town rolling. It is not known where the Halliwell studio found this particular quintet – but they remind us of those odd times so close to us in history when a very significant minority of the town's population was four-legged, and hay and straw were among the community's major imports.

Coal played a very large part in Radcliffe's development, and documentary records and photographs that mark its impact on the community are not hard to find. Yet you need to be close on 70 years old to have much of a recollection of the town's last pit at far-off Outwood, which closed in 1932, while nobody remembers the other dozen, which had all ceased trading by the turn of the century. This is Allens Green Colliery, at the top of Green Street, which bowed to the economic inevitable in 1895.

(*Opposite, top*): Allens Green Colliery tumbled back into the news in the 1950s, when its mineshaft collapsed to the great consternation of the pigs whose sty went down with it. It caused quite a stir around Green Street and Sion Street, and there was much warning of kiddies to stay away. Even the National Coal Board official seen here seems content to keep his investigations at a safe distance.

(*Bottom*): Media interest in the 1950s in Arnold Neely, whose family had made cricket bats for generations. In Edwardian times they had works in Knowles Street and a general sports shop in Church Street.

Waste from open-cast mining between Stopes Road and Radcliffe Moor Road in 1957. It was not a long-lived experiment by the NCB, and there were problems when the excavations went deep enough to break into the underground workings of the old Wilton Colliery.

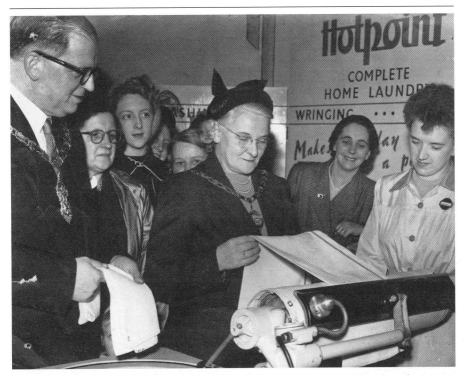

A North Western Electricity Board Try It Yourself promotion in 1953, when the Mayor and Mayoress, Councillor and Mrs J. Isherwood, put a rotary iron to the test. Presumably most people who tried it themselves gave it the thumbs down. When did you last see one of these contraptions?

Stopes Pottery in 1969, shortly before it closed. It was one of the few surviving potteries making chimney cowls, originally using terracotta from just down the road at Ladyshore Colliery in Little Lever. Here the cowls are about to be fired.

Clay pipes and clogs with upturned toes: workers early this century at Samuel Walker's Eagle Iron Works, which specialized in textile mill plant – especially for the bleaching, dyeing, finishing and hat trades.

Foundry workers at Samuel Walker's.

The first cell drier to be patented by Samuel Walker, in 1928, and some of the men behind the success story. Low on steam consumption and especially effective on khaki drills and some rubber products, the driers stood Walker's in good stead for decades.

Esparto grass, shipped in vast quantities up the Manchester Ship Canal to Salford Docks, was a vital raw material at the East Lancashire Paper Mill. Here yet another consignment reaches the works, *c.* 1910.

Paper workers, East Lancashire Paper Mill, *c.* 1920.

Another ELPM group, this time slightly earlier, *c*. 1910.

A superb picture of industry in action in Radcliffe, with paper entering drying cylinders at the East Lancashire Paper Mill in 1954.

High Days and Holidays

Opening the public library in 1907, a boon for the town made possible by a £5,000 donation from the prolific benefactor Andrew Carnegie. Prominent in the centre of the group is County Councillor J.R. Ragdale, an influential figure at the heart of local cultural life.

The library after the fuss had died down, with its close neighbour Bridge Methodist Church. The Methodists' first chapel in this corner of town had stood on the site of the library.

Unveiling the war memorial at the junction of Blackburn Street and Spring Lane on 25 November 1922, the Rev. Heber Marks of St Thomas's church prominent. There must be scores, possibly hundreds, of postcards of this scene tucked away in boxes in Radcliffe, but the one from which this reproduction is taken has an odd little military history of its own. In March 1945 Ken Yates, a young Radcliffe man, was among a group of soldiers who entered the war-devastated town of Radegonde in the Loire region of France. A local woman came forward, asked whether there were any Lancashire lads around – and sure enough, she turned out to be from Radcliffe. Madame Mouvet had an odd tale to tell. She had married a Frenchman in Canada, and by some tragic twist of fate they had found themselves back in his homeland when war broke out. In her middle years, she had found life tough – 'You can't believe what it was like to have the Germans around.' But throughout her hardships she had kept beside her two mementoes of her home town – this picture and another of a long-ago Whit Walk – and she sent them as a present to Mr Yates's mother, who helped track one or two of her remaining relatives.

After the top brass have gone off to tea, the ordinary folk of Radcliffe pay tribute at the new war memorial. Clogs, shawls, and careworn faces: the strain of war shows on these people, and there was no early release from their burdens throughout the hard 1920s and early '30s.

(*Opposite*) 'A Hearty Welcome to all Radcliffe' from the Odeon in 1937, and a goodly number of citizens turned out to pay their respects to the poshest picture house in town. Until then, Radcliffe had had three little neighbourhood cinemas: the Picturedrome, later the Rex, on Water Street, and two tucked away down side streets on either side of Stand Lane, the Coliseum beside the Ambulance Drill Hall in Mellor Street and the Bridge, originally the Palace, beside the Irwell at the junction of River Street and Kenyon Street. Inevitably, by Murphy's Law, it is the scruffiest one of them all that is recalled with most affection today. Those of romantic bent called the Bridge the Ranch, because it showed so many cowboy films. But the more down-to-earth simply knew it as the bug 'ut, and cheerfully asked for 'one and a mallet' – the latter to swat the fleas – as they filed in for a spot of society entertainment.

The platform party at the Radcliffe Literary and Scientific Society's 50th anniversary celebrations in October 1937. It was founded with 57 members in the Golden Jubilee year of 1887, and first president Colonel Mellor gave as his inaugural address a talk on scientific progress during Queen Victoria's reign. The society marked its centenary in 1987, when local historian and former librarian Frank Sunderland was president.

Radcliffe changed its status from an urban district council to a municipal borough on 21 September 1935, and received its charter from King George V from Lord Derby. It rained, of course, but here is the civic party on the balcony of the Town Hall, a building put up with great pride in 1911, described as an 'outstanding edifice' in the charter celebration brochure – and today a sadly neglected and derelict outpost superfluous to Bury Metro Council's needs.

The Charter Ball. Charter Mayor was John Seddon, not a local politician but then managing director of the East Lancashire Paper Mill. He succeeded his illustrious father Charles Robert Seddon as chairman when the elder man died in 1939, and was in turn succeeded by his son Charles Geoffrey when he passed on in 1947. One slight irony of his mayoralty was the fact that he was a Whitefield resident.

More rain, top hats aplenty and another big day for Charter Mayor John Seddon on Civic Sunday, 1935. The bewigged town clerk was the long-serving Sam Mills.

John Seddon's deputy as Charter Mayor was council chairman Harry Makin, left, then Councillor and later Alderman, a lifelong local politician who was still active until comparatively recent times.

Norman Street, now itself a part of history, won the street decoration contest at the 1953 Coronation. It's not hard to see why, though in truth hundreds of streets put in just as much effort, perhaps not to quite such good effect. Norman Street was lucky to have that end wall on which to weave that added little bit of magic.

The name of Bealey was known in Radcliffe for both bleaching and philanthropy for well over two hundred years. The family ran their bleach works with an air of enlightened paternalism, and it is certain that many readers of this book took their first breaths at Bealey Maternity Hospital, now Bury Hospice. This picture from 1913 shows Miss Mary Bealey making a presentation of a brass microscope to A.C. Bealey and Son's works manager, Mr Smith.

Dobson and Barlow at Bradley Fold was one of several companies of world-wide repute of which Radcliffe was justly proud. The Queen set the seal on their standing with a visit in May 1968, and here she signs the visitors' book watched by Sir Kenneth Preston, chairman of Stone-Platt Industries, and works managing director Mr W. Thornley. After such high-profile endorsement, what could possibly go wrong?

All that could be said of Dobson and Barlow applied at least as much to their neighbours Mather and Platt. Here the Prince of Swaziland pays a visit in 1974, while his aide makes earnest notes.

Commemorative mugs, a handsome cake and smiling faces: neighbours in and around Sycamore and Beech Avenues, Outwood, celebrate the Queen's Silver Jubilee in 1977.

A pioneering cinema comes to Radcliffe in the shape of Kemp and Son's Famous Electric Theatre.

All dressed up, and a sunny day. An East Lancashire Paper Mill social gathering in the 1920s.

This Sporting Life

Radcliffe Rugby Club, turn of the century.

Ainsworth Road Football Club, pre-1914.

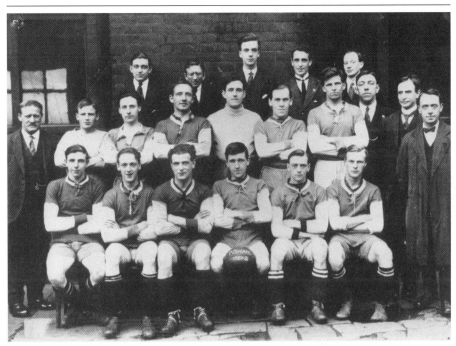

Bridge Wesleyan Methodist Church Football Club, 1921–2. Tie-strings around the collar became a revived fashion fad for several major clubs in the early 1990s.

Radcliffe St John's Football Club, 1946–7, winners of the Bury Sunday School League and the Walter Spencer Cup three years in a row – on either side of the war.

Cheerful, friendly faces, but you wouldn't want to get on the wrong side of them. Radcliffe Swimming Club water polo team at Whittaker Street, 1935.

The water polo team in 1971: short shorts and snazzy hats, but the physical require-
ments of the sport seem very much the same.

Huntsman Reid toots his horn to lead the Holcombe Hunt away from the Black Bull in 1964.

Nellie Halstead of Radcliffe, who died in the early 1990s, was a cheery Bury Athletics Club star who represented Britain in the 1930 World Games and the 1932 and '36 Olympics, and was the British champion at 100, 220 and 440 yards. The picture below shows her beating Dollinger of Germany in a 200 metres race in Florence at the height of her powers in 1931.

Lads from Radcliffe's Excelsior Cycle Club celebrate their arrival at Blackpool with a visit to Will Cooper's photographic studio in Wellington Terrace in 1935. The occasion was memorable for another reason – it was George V's Silver Jubilee day.

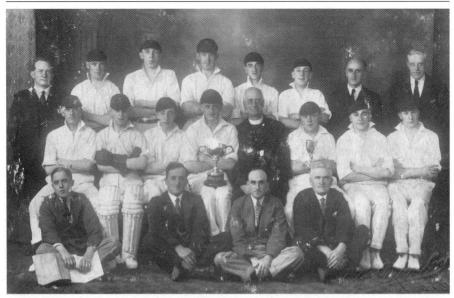

St John's church ran two formidable cricket teams in the inter-war years, and was always a force to be reckoned with in the Radcliffe Sunday School League. This picture shows the first team, *c.* 1930.

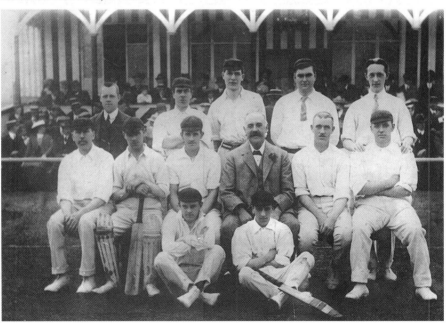

There was something special about that long, hot summer of 1914 – not least for Radcliffe Cricket Club, who did the double by winning the Bolton and District Cricket Association League and Cup.

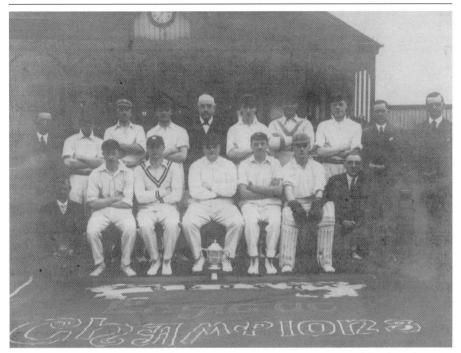

The Radcliffe team did the Bolton Association Double again in 1928, knocking up 2,560 League runs in the process. The championship flag in the foreground adds to the sense of occasion.

Championships have come to the Racecourse – until 1876 it was just that – reasonably frequently in the Radcliffe club's long history. This is the 1944 side that topped the Central Lancashire League and reached the Wood Cup final.

The West Indian legend Garfield Sobers was just 21 when he joined Radcliffe as a professional in 1958, but already he was a force in the cricket world, with a record Test innings of 365 under his belt. A star with both the bat and the ball, he promptly helped the team to championship success, a feat never achieved by his illustrious countryman Frank Worrell, pro for a number of seasons in the early 1950s. As for that innings of 365, it remained a Test record until it was broken by another young West Indies star, Brian Lara, who scored 375 against England in April 1994.

The Aussie Cec Pepper was pro at the Racecourse from 1954 to 1956. It wasn't easy following on from Worrell, but his feats included a club record breaking 176 in 1955, when he also broke the 1,000 runs and 100 wickets barrier for the season.

Garfield Sobers in his later playing years. The Racecourse buzzed with the feats of the great West Indians in the 1950s, and now a corner of the pavilion bar commemorates the contribution to the club of Worrell, Sobers and a later Test player, Ezra Moseley.

It started as just another game, Middleton against Radcliffe in a Central Lancashire League fixture in May 1952. But it rewrote the club's record book, with opening batsmen Frank Worrell and Billy Greenhalgh running up unbeaten innings of 152 and 144 respectively. The fact that there were only seven extras says much for the way the Middleton bowlers and wicketkeeper stuck to their task. And the fact that Greenhalgh all but matched the great Worrell, at the peak of his form, says much about the quality of League cricket in Lancashire at that time. Worrell was a devastating run-maker, hitting just six short of 1,700 in 1951.

The Radcliffe St John's Junior School soccer team that won the Scholes Cup in 1934. The little skipper with the cup and ball might have had something to do with it. Johnny Morris went on to play for England and help Manchester United win the FA Cup in 1948. Related to another Radcliffe soccer hero, Eddie Quigley, he still lives in the town.

Acknowledgements

Thanks for the loan of pictures, background information and other help are due to:

Maxine Armitage • Terry Atherton • Jim Barlow • John Carter
Co-Operative Union Ltd • Vera Duerdin • The East Lancashire Paper Mill
The Rev. Charles Ellis • Yvonne Evans • John and Margaret Fletcher
Tim Gavell • Philip Gooderson • Alice Hardman • Jack Heathcote
Phyllis Hudson • Rod Launders • Dorothy Lindsay • Gillian Lonergan
The Manchester, Bolton & Bury Canal Society • Sylvia Mason
Radcliffe Cricket Club • Radcliffe Library staff, and donors of photographs
to the library collection • The *Radcliffe Times* • Diana Sorrigan • Irene Thorp
Frank Sunderland • Ken Yates